confirming

your faith

{STUDENT JOURNAL}

by Jim Burns

Group

Loveland, Colorado

R.E.A.L. Guarantee to you:

This Group resource incorporates our R.E.A.L. approach to ministry—one that encourages long-term retention and life transformation. It's ministry that's:

Relational
Because learner-to-learner interaction enhances learning and builds Christian friendships.

Experiential
Because what learners experience through discussion and action sticks with them up to 9 times longer than what they simply hear or read.

Applicable
Because the aim of Christian education is to equip learners to be both hearers and doers of God's Word.

Learner-based
Because learners understand and retain more when the learning process takes into consideration how they learn best.

Confirming Your Faith

STUDENT JOURNAL

Copyright © 2003 Jim Burns

Visit our Web site: **www.grouppublishing.com**

For more about YouthBuilders, check out www.youthbuilders.com

CREDITS

Acquisitions Editor: *Amy Simpson*	Book Designer: *Jean Bruns*
Editor: *Paul Woods*	Print Production Artist: *Joyce Douglas*
Creative Development Editor: *Dave Thornton*	Cover Art Director and Designer: *Jeff A. Storm*
Chief Creative Officer: *Joani Schultz*	Cover Photographer: *Daniel Treat*
Copy Editor: *Linda Marcinkowski*	Production Manager: *Peggy Naylor*

Unless otherwise noted, Scripture taken from the HOLY BIBLE, NEW INTERNATIONAL VERSION®. Copyright © 1973, 1978, 1984 by International Bible Society. Used by permission of Zondervan Publishing House. All rights reserved.

ISBN 0-7644-2587-0
10 9 8 7 6 5 4 3 2 1   12 11 10 09 08 07 06 05 04 03
Printed in the United States of America.

Dedication

To Christy Meredith Burns

You made it! You have successfully moved from childhood to adulthood. One of the greatest days of my life was the day you were born. Through the years, observing the incredibly great decisions you have made about your life and faith continues to bring me more joy than I can ever describe to you. You are an inspiration. I love you and I'm proud of you.

Dad

Acknowledgements

Thanks and thanks again...

To my wife, Cathy. You have stood beside me with so much support.

To my daughters—Christy, Rebecca, and Heidi. You are making wise decisions with your rites of passage. I'm honored to be your dad.

To Carrie. Your devotion to your husband, family, and this ministry is nothing short of amazing. You are a gift.

To the YouthBuilders staff and board. Your dedication to help adults help kids is what keeps me going. I am so fortunate to work alongside you.

To Group Publishing. Thom and Joani, you have led the way and multiplied your ministry to thousands. Amy Simpson and Kelli Trujillo, you are wonderful people and wonderful editors. We gave birth to this project at a very special season in life. Congratulations.

Introduction

A JOURNAL FOR YOUR JOURNEY

You are on the most amazing journey of your life—called adolescence—and just as you are changing and growing in other ways, so is your faith in God. This journal is designed to help you as you embark on this very special journey of faith. It's a place to write out your thoughts, your prayers, your questions, your hopes, and your dreams. Pursue this journey with energy and enthusiasm. If you do, your life will be far from boring. It will be an adventure that will take you far beyond what you have imagined in life, and God will walk with you every step of the way.

Jim Burns, Ph.D.
President, YouthBuilders
www.youthbuilders.com

How to Use This Journal

The sessions in this journal connect with the topics covered in the *Confirming Your Faith Leaders Guide*. This is your spot to write what you want and explore faith questions on your own or with a spiritual-growth partner. Each session is divided into five parts:

Scripture Reading

Here you'll take a few moments and read, reflect, and respond to the Word of God.

Inspirational Thoughts

These quotes from other Christians are for reading and reflection. You can just read them or comment on them.

Prayers / Hopes / Dreams

Many people communicate better in writing than verbally. Try writing down your prayers, hopes, and dreams as you journey with God and watch him work in your life.

Going Deeper

In this section you can take the topic to the next level through an experience, a verse to memorize, or an extra impact activity. Give it a try.

Checking In

This section encourages you to keep yourself accountable. Spiritual accountability can be a very powerful tool for spiritual growth. Choose an accountability partner or mentor for this series. Write out your answers to the "Things to Think About" section from your group session, and share them with your spiritual-growth partner. Have fun and be willing to put your life in God's hands.

{ Section One }

what I
believe

THE APOSTLES' CREED: I BELIEVE

The Apostles' Creed

I believe in God, the Father Almighty, Maker of heaven and earth; and in Jesus Christ, His only Son, our Lord; who was conceived by the Holy Spirit, born of the Virgin Mary, suffered under Pontius Pilate, was crucified, died and was buried. He descended into hell. The third day He rose again from the dead. He ascended into heaven and sits at the right hand of God, the Father Almighty. From thence He will come to judge the living and the dead. I believe in the Holy Spirit, the holy Christian Church, the communion of saints, the forgiveness of sins, the resurrection of the body, and the life everlasting. Amen.

Scripture Reading

Jesus said to her, "I am the resurrection and the life. He who believes in me will live, even though he dies; and whoever lives and believes in me will never die. Do you believe this?"

"Yes, Lord," she told him, "I believe that you are the Christ, the Son of God, who was to come into the world."

JOHN 11:25-27

▷ Read

What are the key thoughts of this Scripture?

_____

_____

_____

_____

_____

_____

▷ Reflect

reflect

How does this Scripture speak to me personally?

_____

_____

_____

_____

_____

_____

▷ Respond

What truths can I put into practice?

_____

_____

_____

_____

_____

_____

_____

RESPOND

"I am trying here to prevent anyone saying the really foolish thing that people often say about Him: 'I'm ready to accept Jesus as a great moral teacher, but I don't accept His claim to be God.' "

–C.S. Lewis, *Mere Christianity*

inspirational thought

Going Deeper

Memorizing the Apostles' Creed is a great step toward putting good things in your mind. Just like learning and memorizing the words to your favorite songs, you will learn the Apostles' Creed by saying it over and over again. Learn it a phrase at a time, and before you know it, these awesome words of your faith will be forever in your mind and heart.

CHECKING IN

We often learn best through interaction and action. Write out your answers and then use these questions as dialogue with an accountability partner or mentor. (See instructions in section on How to Use This Journal, page 5.)

1. *Why is it important to have a solid knowledge of what we believe?*

2. *How are the three works of the Apostles' Creed (creation, redemption, sanctification) similar to the Trinity?*

3. *What does something like the Apostles' Creed have to do with our everyday living at home, school and church?*

THE TEN COMMANDMENTS

Scripture Reading

The Ten Commandments

1.
You shall have no other gods before me.

2.
You shall not make for yourself an idol.

3.
You shall not misuse the name
of the Lord your God.

4.
Remember the Sabbath day
by keeping it holy.

5.
Honor your father and your mother.

6.
You shall not murder.

7.
You shall not commit adultery.

8.
You shall not steal.

9.
You shall not give false testimony
against your neighbor.

10.
You shall not covet...anything that
belongs to your neighbor.

(ADAPTED FROM EXODUS 20:3-17)

▶ Read

What are the key thoughts of this Scripture?

_____

_____

_____

_____

_____

_____

▶ Reflect

reflect

How does this Scripture speak to me personally?

_____

_____

_____

_____

_____

_____

▶ Respond

What truths can I put into practice?

_____

_____

_____

_____

_____

_____

RESPOND

"If you truly want God to give you your life back, you must begin to pay attention to the 'Do Not Enter' signs posted in front of certain behaviors, thought patterns, and attitudes."

—Gary Thomas,
The Glorious Pursuit

inspirational thought

Going Deeper

Memorize the Ten Commandments. (You should already have a jump on memorizing them since you memorized two in the last session.) They're pretty short, so it shouldn't take too much time!

CHECKING IN

1. Do you think most people break at least one of the commandments every single day? Why or why not?

2. What would Jesus say about the breaking of commandments?

3. What makes living by God's laws difficult?

THE LORD'S PRAYER

Scripture Reading

The Lord's Prayer

Our Father in heaven,
hallowed be your name,
your kingdom come,
your will be done
on earth as it is in heaven.
Give us today our daily bread.
Forgive us our debts,
as we also have forgiven our debtors.
And lead us not into temptation,
but deliver us from the evil one.

MATTHEW 6:9-13

▶ Read

What are the key thoughts of this Scripture?

_____

_____

_____

_____

_____

_____

_____

▶ Reflect

reflect

How does this Scripture speak to me personally?

_____

_____

_____

_____

_____

_____

▶ Respond

What truths can I put into practice?

_____

_____

_____

_____

_____

_____

RESPOND

inspirational thought

"The first and chief need of our Christian life is, Fellowship with God."

—Andrew Murray,
The Deeper Christian Life

"Prayerless people cut themselves off from God's prevailing power, and the frequent result is the familiar feeling of being overwhelmed, overrun, beaten down, pushed around, defeated...Prayer is the key to unlocking God's prevailing power in your life."

—Bill Hybels,
Too Busy Not to Pray

Going Deeper

If you don't already have it memorized, memorize the Lord's Prayer. It's a good prayer to have in the back of your mind at any time!

> "Our Father in heaven, hallowed be your name, your kingdom come, your will be done on earth as it is in heaven. Give us today our daily bread. Forgive us our debts, as we also have forgiven our debtors. And lead us not into temptation, but deliver us from the evil one" (Matthew 6:9-13).

Read the story of Jesus in the Garden of Gethsemane (Matthew 26:36-46). Here Jesus prays a prayer of relinquishment to God, "not as I will, but as you will."

• How is this prayer similar to the Lord's Prayer?

• What part of your will do you need to relinquish or turn over to God?

CHECKING IN

1. *What makes this prayer important?*

2. *Why do you think Jesus took the time to teach his followers to pray?*

3. *What aspect of this prayer is most meaningful to you right now?*

BAPTISM

Scripture Reading

Then Jesus came from Galilee to the Jordan to be baptized by John. But John tried to deter him, saying, "I need to be baptized by you, and do you come to me?"

Jesus replied, "Let it be so now; it is proper for us to do this to fulfill all righteousness." Then John consented.

As soon as Jesus was baptized, he went up out of the water. At that moment heaven was opened, and he saw the Spirit of God descending like a dove and lighting on him. And a voice from heaven said, "This is my Son, whom I love; with him I am well pleased."

MATTHEW 3:13-17

Peter replied, "Repent and be baptized, every one of you, in the name of Jesus Christ for the forgiveness of your sins. And you will receive the gift of the Holy Spirit. The promise is for you and your children and for all who are far off—for all whom the Lord our God will call."

ACTS 2:38-39

20

▷ Read

What are the key thoughts of this Scripture?

▷ Reflect

reflect

How does this Scripture speak to me personally?

▷ Respond

What truths can I put into practice?

RESPOND

"Baptism is not just plain water, but it is the water included in God's command and combined with God's word...It means that in Baptism, God, the Holy Trinity, receives me into communion or fellowship with Himself."

—Martin Luther,
Luther's Small Catechism

inspirational thought

Going Deeper

Memorize Acts 2:38 to help you recall the significance of baptism.

> "Peter replied, 'Repent and be baptized, every one of you, in the name of Jesus Christ for the forgiveness of your sins. And you will receive the gift of the Holy Spirit' " (Acts 2:38).

Read John 3:1-21.

• Why did Jesus come into our world?

_____

_____

• What in this story and teaching relates to what you learned about baptism?

_____

_____

1. What makes the simple act of baptism so meaningful?

_____

_____

_____

_____

_____

_____

2. According to Matthew 3:13-17, why did Jesus get baptized?

_____

_____

_____

_____

_____

3. Why is it important to have family and friends involved with our baptism?

_____

_____

_____

_____

(Session Four) BAPTISM

COMMUNION

Scripture Reading

For I received from the Lord what I also passed on to you: The Lord Jesus, on the night he was betrayed, took bread, and when he had given thanks, he broke it and said, "This is my body, which is for you; do this in remembrance of me." In the same way, after supper he took the cup, saying, "This cup is the new covenant in my blood; do this, whenever you drink it, in remembrance of me."

1 CORINTHIANS 11:23-25

▷ Read

What are the key thoughts of this Scripture?

▷ Reflect

reflect

How does this Scripture speak to me personally?

▷ Respond

What truths can I put into practice?

RESPOND

"To embrace God's love and kingdom is to embrace his broken, passionate heart."

—Gary Thomas, *Authentic Faith*

"When we received forgiveness instead of judgment, we, too, were made ready to forgive our brethren. What God did to us, we then owed to others. The more we received, the more we were able to give; and the more meager our brotherly love, the less were we living by God's mercy and love."

—Dietrich Bonhoeffer, *Life Together*

"It is worth any sacrifice to do the will of God; it is worth any surgical excision from life, of your desires and your ambitions and your plans and your aims, to do the will of God."

—William Barclay, *The Life of Jesus for Everyman*

Going Deeper

Read Exodus 12, the story of the Passover. Jot down some of the similarities between the Passover experience and meal and our celebration of communion. If you have questions, don't hesitate to talk to your youth leader or pastor.

• Why is it important for us to celebrate communion?

CHECKING IN

1. *Why do you think Jesus used the celebration of the Passover to talk about his sacrificial death?*

2. *Why is Romans 5:8 such a good summary of this event?*

3. *What must we all do as we prepare to take communion?*

{ Section Two }

my
commitments

THE CHURCH

Scripture Reading

And let us consider how we may spur one another on toward love and good deeds. Let us not give up meeting together, as some are in the habit of doing, but let us encourage one another—and all the more as you see the Day approaching.

HEBREWS 10:24-25

And God placed all things under his feet and appointed him to be head over everything for the church, which is his body, the fullness of him who fills everything in every way.

EPHESIANS 1:22-23

▷ Read

What are the key thoughts of this Scripture?

_____

_____

_____

_____

_____

_____

▷ Reflect

reflect

How does this Scripture speak to me personally?

_____

_____

_____

_____

_____

_____

▷ Respond

What truths can I put into practice?

_____

_____

_____

_____

_____

_____

_____

"God always uses imperfect people in imperfect situations to accomplish his will."

—Rick Warren,
The Purpose-Driven Church

"The local church is the hope of the world. The local church is the hope of the world."

—Bill Hybels,
Courageous Leadership

Going Deeper

Take a few minutes to memorize Hebrews 10:24-25.

> "And let us consider how we may spur one another on toward love and good deeds. Let us not give up meeting together, as some are in the habit of doing, but let us encourage one another—and all the more as you see the Day approaching" (Hebrews 10:24-25).

Read 1 Corinthians 12:12-30. How does this illustration of the body of Christ relate to you personally in your relationship with the church?

1. What's the best thing about your church?

2. If you were the pastor of your church, what would you try to change?

3. What can a young person do to feel more a part of the entire church body?

PROFESSING YOUR FAITH

Scripture Reading

That if you confess with your mouth, "Jesus is Lord," and believe in your heart that God raised him from the dead, you will be saved. For it is with your heart that you believe and are justified, and it is with your mouth that you confess and are saved.

ROMANS 10:9-10

▶ Read

What are the key thoughts of this Scripture?

_____
_____
_____
_____
_____
_____
_____

▶ Reflect

How does this Scripture speak to me personally?

_____
_____
_____
_____
_____
_____

▶ Respond

What truths can I put into practice?

_____
_____
_____
_____
_____
_____
_____

"Knowing the heart of Jesus and loving him are the same thing. The knowledge of Jesus' heart is a knowledge of the heart. And when we live in the world with that knowledge, we cannot do other than bring healing, reconciliation, new life, and hope wherever we go."

—Henri J.M. Nouwen,
In the Name of Jesus

Jesus was a dangerous man—dangerous to the power structure...Shouldn't the *followers* of Christ also be dangerous?...Shouldn't Christians be known by the fire in their souls, the wild-eyed gratitude in their faces, the twinkle in their eyes...Shouldn't those who call themselves Christians be filled with awe, astonishment, and amazement?

—Mike Yaconelli,
Dangerous Wonder

Going Deeper

Memorize Romans 10:9-10.

> *"That if you confess with your mouth, 'Jesus is Lord,' and believe in your heart that God raised him from the dead, you will be saved. For it is with your heart that you believe and are justified, and it is with your mouth that you confess and are saved"* (Romans 10:9-10).

Read Deuteronomy 6:4-6. This is the Jewish profession of faith.

• How is it similar to the Christian profession of faith?

_____

_____

• What did Jesus say about this profession in Mark 12:28-31?

_____

_____

1. *Do you have to understand everything about God to profess belief in him?*

_____

_____

_____

_____

2. *What would you say are the important elements of a solid profession of faith?*

_____

_____

_____

3. *Who do you feel comfortable professing your faith to?*

_____

_____

_____

_____

PURITY

Scripture Reading

Flee from sexual immorality. All other sins a man commits are outside his body, but he who sins sexually sins against his own body. Do you not know that your body is a temple of the Holy Spirit, who is in you, whom you have received from God? You are not your own; you were bought at a price. Therefore honor God with your body.

1 CORINTHIANS 6:18-20

▶ Read

What are the key thoughts of this Scripture?

▶ Reflect

How does this Scripture speak to me personally?

▶ Respond

What truths can I put into practice?

inspirational thought

> "We can then say that chastity—biblical love, sexual purity, and marital fidelity—is right for all people, for all times, for all places."
>
> —Josh McDowell and
> Bob Hostetler,
> *Right From Wrong*

> "As you embrace your sexuality, do so with self-control, sanctity, high esteem, lovingly and not lustfully, sacrificially and not 'wronging' someone, and in submission to God."
>
> —Dr. Henry Cloud and
> Dr. John Townsend,
> *Boundaries in Dating*

Going Deeper

Memorize 1 Corinthians 6:20. This one should be easy!

"You were bought at a price. Therefore honor God with your body"
(1 Corinthians 6:20).

Read 1 Thessalonians 4:3.

• How does this Scripture relate to this generation?

_____

_____

• How does it relate to you?

_____

_____

CHECKING IN

1. *What makes living a life of purity so difficult for this generation?*

_____

_____

2. *Why is accountability an important ingredient to keeping pure?*

_____

_____

3. *When it comes to honoring God with our bodies, how significant are friends? church? Internet? movies? parties?*

_____

_____

TIME WITH GOD

Scripture Reading

This is the day the Lord has made; let us rejoice and be glad in it.

PSALM 118:24

Your word is a lamp to my feet and a light for my path.

PSALM 119:105

Read

What are the key thoughts of this Scripture?

Reflect

How does this Scripture speak to me personally?

Respond

What truths can I put into practice?

"If you are too busy to pray, you are too busy."

—Bill Hybels

"To live a Christian life means to live *in* the world without being *of* it. It is in solitude that this inner freedom can grow. Jesus went to a lonely place to pray...to grow in the awareness that all the power he had was given to him... from his Father."

—Henri J. M. Nouwen,
Out of Solitude

"Prayer is two-way fellowship and communication with God. You speak to God and He speaks to you. It is not a one-way conversation...Prayer includes listening as well. In fact, what God says in prayer is far more important than what you say."

—Henry T. Blackaby and
Claude V. King,
Experiencing God

Going Deeper

Memorize Psalm 118:24—another short and easy one!

"This is the day the Lord has made; let us rejoice and be glad in it" (Psalm 118:24).

Read James 4:7-8.

• What is the point and the promise in this Scripture?

CHECKING IN

1. Why is it difficult to have the discipline to spend time daily with God?

2. What point from the D.A.I.L.Y. study made the biggest impression on you?

3. How will accountability help keep you focused on living out your Christian commitment?

{ Section Three }

God
using me

SPIRITUAL GIFTS

Scripture Reading

There are different kinds of gifts, but the same Spirit. There are different kinds of service, but the same Lord. There are different kinds of working, but the same God works all of them in all men.

Now to each one the manifestation of the Spirit is given for the common good. To one there is given through the Spirit the message of wisdom, to another the message of knowledge by means of the same Spirit, to another faith by the same Spirit, to another gifts of healing by that one Spirit, to another miraculous powers, to another prophecy, to another distinguishing between spirits, to another speaking in different kinds of tongues, and to still another the interpretation of tongues. All these are the work of one and the same Spirit, and he gives them to each one, just as he determines.

1 CORINTHIANS 12:4-11

▷ Read

What are the key thoughts of this Scripture?

_____

_____

_____

_____

_____

_____

_____

▷ Reflect

reflect

How does this Scripture speak to me personally?

_____

_____

_____

_____

_____

_____

▷ Respond

What truths can I put into practice?

_____

_____

_____

_____

_____

_____

_____

_____

RESPOND

"What happens when you decide to discover, develop, and use your spiritual gift or gifts?...you will be a better Christian and more able to allow God to make your life count for Him."

—C. Peter Wagner, *Your Spiritual Gifts Can Help Your Church Grow*

"Christian students have not only been invited to play in the game of ministry, they have been given the equipment to play well...I love to say, 'Congratulations, you're gifted!' It is wonderful to see their eyes get big when they find out that God has gifted every believer."

—Doug Fields, *Purpose-Driven Youth Ministry*

Going Deeper

Memorize 1 Corinthians 7:7. It's a great reminder!

> *"I wish that all men were as I am. But each man has his own gift from God; one has this gift, another has that"* (1 Corinthians 7:7).

Read Romans 12:1-8.

• What does this section of Scripture have to say about your life and your spiritual gifts?

_____

_____

• What might be the most likely way for you to exercise a spiritual gift you've discovered?

_____

_____

CHECKING IN

1. *What makes learning about spiritual gifts confusing?*

_____

_____

_____

_____

2. *What makes discovering your spiritual gifts exciting?*

_____

_____

_____

_____

3. *What other questions do you have about finding and using your spiritual gifts?*

_____

_____

_____

SERVANTHOOD

Scripture Reading

When the Son of Man comes in his glory, and all the angels with him, he will sit on his throne in heavenly glory. All the nations will be gathered before him, and he will separate the people one from another as a shepherd separates the sheep from the goats. He will put the sheep on his right and the goats on his left.

Then the King will say to those on his right, "Come, you who are blessed by my Father; take your inheritance, the kingdom prepared for you since the creation of the world. For I was hungry and you gave me something to eat, I was thirsty and you gave me something to drink, I was a stranger and you invited me in, I needed clothes and you clothed me, I was sick and you looked after me, I was in prison and you came to visit me."

Then the righteous will answer him, "Lord, when did we see you hungry and feed you, or thirsty and give you something to drink? When did we see you a stranger and invite you in or needing clothes and clothe you? When did we see you sick or in prison and go to visit you?"

The King will reply, "I tell you the truth, whatever you did for one of the least of these brothers of mine, you did for me."

Then he will say to those on his left, "Depart from me, you who are cursed, into the eternal fire prepared for the devil and his angels. For I was hungry and you gave me nothing to eat, I was thirsty and you gave me nothing to drink, I was a stranger and you did not invite me in, I needed clothes and you did not clothe me, I was sick and in prison and you did not look after me."

They also will answer, "Lord, when did we see you hungry or thirsty or a stranger or needing clothes or sick or in prison, and did not help you?"

He will reply, "I tell you the truth, whatever you did not do for one of the least of these, you did not do for me."

Then they will go away to eternal punishment, but the righteous to eternal life.

MATTHEW 25:31-46

Read

What are the key thoughts of this Scripture?

Reflect

How does this Scripture speak to me personally?

Respond

What truths can I put into practice?

"When Jesus came in the form of a servant, he was not disguising who God is. He was revealing who God is."

—John Ortberg,
The Life You've Always Wanted

"Service must take form and shape in the world in which we live. Therefore we must seek to perceive what service may look like in the marketplace of our daily lives."

—Richard J. Foster,
Celebration of Discipline

Going Deeper

Memorize Luke 22:27. These are words of Jesus, the Son of God.

> "For who is greater, the one who is at the table or the one who serves? Is it not the one who is at the table? But I am among you as one who serves" (Luke 22:27).

Read Luke 9:46-48.

- What did Jesus mean when he said, "For he who is least among you all—he is the greatest"?

_____

_____

- How does this apply to your life?

_____

_____

CHECKING IN

1. Is there a difference between a servant and a leader? Explain.

_____

_____

_____

2. Why did Jesus become a servant even when he was the Son of God?

_____

_____

_____

3. What makes the idea of servanthood extra-appealing in today's "me-first" society?

_____

_____

_____

_____

{ Session Eleven } SERVANTHOOD

Scripture Reading

Hear, O Israel: The Lord our God, the Lord is one. Love the Lord your God with all your heart and with all your soul and with all your strength. These commandments that I give you today are to be upon your hearts. Impress them on your children. Talk about them when you sit at home and when you walk along the road, when you lie down and when you get up. Tie them as symbols on your hands and bind them on your foreheads. Write them on the doorframes of your houses and on your gates.

DEUTERONOMY 6:4-9

Read

What are the key thoughts of this Scripture?

Reflect

reflect

How does this Scripture speak to me personally?

Respond

What truths can I put into practice?

"Family is a big deal to teenagers, regardless of how they act or what they say. It is the rare teenager who believes he or she can lead a fulfilling life without receiving complete acceptance and support from his or her family."

—George Barna, *Real Teens*

"A hundred years from now it will not matter what my bank account was, the sort of house I lived in, or the kind of car I drove, but the world may be different because I was important in the life of a child."

—Author unknown

inspirational thought

Going Deeper

Memorize Ephesians 6:1-3. It will honor your parents...and God!

> "Children, obey your parents in the Lord, for this is right. 'Honor your father and mother'—which is the first commandment with a promise—'that it may go well with you and that you may enjoy long life on the earth' " (Ephesians 6:1-3).

Read Exodus 20:12.

• What is the promise in this commandment?

_____

_____

• What do you think it means you should do?

_____

_____

CHECKING IN

1. Read the reply Jesus gave to the Jewish leaders in Matthew 22:34-40. What did he say concerning the Shema?

_____

_____

_____

2. What makes the spiritual legacy concept so much a part of our rites of passage and confirming our faith?

_____

_____

3. What should students do who hope to pass on a spiritual legacy but who do not have parents that are active in the Christian faith?

_____

_____

_____

{ Session Twelve } FAMILY

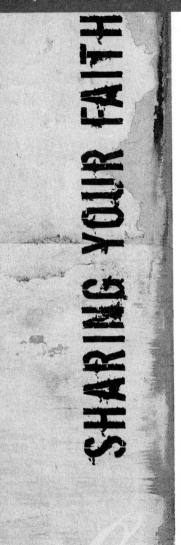

SHARING YOUR FAITH

Scripture Reading

Then Agrippa said to Paul, "You have permission to speak for yourself." So Paul motioned with his hand and began his defense: "King Agrippa, I consider myself fortunate to stand before you today as I make my defense against all the accusations of the Jews, and especially so because you are well acquainted with all the Jewish customs and controversies. Therefore, I beg you to listen to me patiently.

"The Jews all know the way I have lived ever since I was a child, from the beginning of my life in my own country, and also in Jerusalem. They have known me for a long time and can testify, if they are willing, that according to the strictest sect of our religion, I lived as a Pharisee. And now it is because of my hope in what God has promised our fathers that I am on trial today. This is the promise our twelve tribes are hoping to see fulfilled as they earnestly serve God day and night. O king, it is because of this hope that the Jews are accusing me. Why should any of you consider it incredible that God raises the dead?

"I too was convinced that I ought to do all that was possible to oppose the name of Jesus of Nazareth. And that is just what I did in Jerusalem. On the authority of the chief priests I put many of the saints in prison, and when they were put to death, I cast my vote against them. Many a time I went from one synagogue to another to have them punished, and I tried to force them to blaspheme. In my obsession against them, I even went to foreign cities to persecute them.

"On one of these journeys I was going to Damascus with the authority and commission of the chief priests. About noon, O king, as I was on the road, I saw a light from heaven, brighter than the sun, blazing around me and my companions. We all fell to the ground, and I heard a voice saying to me in Aramaic, 'Saul, Saul, why do you persecute me? It is hard for you to kick against the goads.'

"Then I asked, 'Who are you, Lord?'

" 'I am Jesus, whom you are persecuting,' the Lord replied. 'Now get up and stand on your feet. I have appeared to you to appoint you as a servant and as a witness of what you have seen of me and what I will show you. I will rescue you from your own people and from the Gentiles. I am sending you to them to open their eyes and turn them from darkness to light, and from the power of Satan to God, so that they may receive forgiveness of sins and a place among those who are sanctified by faith in me.'

"So then, King Agrippa, I was not disobedient to the vision from heaven. First to those in Damascus, then to those in Jerusalem and in all Judea, and to the Gentiles also, I preached that they should repent and turn to God and prove their repentance by their deeds. That is why the Jews seized me in the temple courts and tried to kill me. But I have had God's help to this very day, and so I stand here and testify to small and great alike. I am saying nothing beyond what the prophets and Moses said would happen— that the Christ would suffer and, as the first to rise from the dead, would proclaim light to his own people and to the Gentiles."

ACTS 26:1-23

Read

What are the key thoughts of this Scripture?

Reflect

reflect

How does this Scripture speak to me personally?

Respond

What truths can I put into practice?

"Even after generations of people had spit in his face, he still loved them. After a nation of chosen ones had stripped him naked and ripped his incarnated flesh, he still died for them. And even today, after billions have chosen to prostitute themselves...he still waits for them."

—Max Lucado,
God Came Near

"What we must not forget is that we [Christians] incarnate Jesus! Whatever our life intersects with, so does Jesus. Whomever we touch, Jesus touches. We do not simply give the gospel, we are the gospel."

—Rebecca Manley Pippert,
*Out of the Saltshaker &
Into the World*

inspirational thought

Going Deeper

Memorize John 3:16-17. This one is probably already familiar to you.

> "For God so loved the world that he gave his one and only Son, that whoever believes in him shall not perish but have eternal life. For God did not send his Son into the world to condemn the world, but to save the world through him" (John 3:16-17).

Read 1 Thessalonians 2:8.

• What does this verse say about sharing the gospel?

_____

_____

• How can we share with others not only the gospel, but our lives?

_____

_____

CHECKING IN

1. What makes sharing your story with a non-believer an often-scary experience?

_____

_____

_____

2. Why is the story of God sending his Son to die for humankind so that we can have eternal life still hard to communicate to the world?

_____

_____

_____

3. What makes telling your story more effective than preaching a sermon or leading a Bible study?

_____

_____

_____